Thoughts on the Proposed Inclosure of Waltham (commonly called Epping) and Hainault Forests

In which a new plan is suggested for disafforesting the same: with the heads of the bill now proposed for that purpose

Thomas Street

Alpha Editions

This edition published in 2023

ISBN : 9789357947183

Design and Setting By
Alpha Editions
www.alphaedis.com
Email - info@alphaedis.com

Contents

TO THE LORDS OF MANORS, FREEHOLDERS, COPYHOLDERS, AND OTHER OWNERS OF LANDED PROPERTY, SITUATE WITHIN THE BOUNDARIES OF WALTHAM AND HAINAULT FORESTS.

GENTLEMEN,

WHEN I took the liberty of addressing you, in January last, on the subject of the projected inclosure of these Forests, I could not foresee that the plan I submitted to general consideration would have been adopted by the Commissioners of Woods and Forests, which it appears, by the Heads of the Bill, they now propose bringing into Parliament has been done; and the giving effect to a plan, on the mere suggestion of a private individual, whose name was not even known to them, shews, on their part, the strongest desire, in executing the duties of their office, to afford every possible degree of accommodation to the interest and convenience of the persons to be affected by it. Connected as I am with gentlemen who have considerable property in these Forests, I do earnestly hope that the plan I have suggested, and which has been, on the part of the Commissioners of Woods and Forests, so liberally adopted, will be carried into effect; and, at the request of several friends, I have been induced to re-publish my Thoughts on the subject, in the hope that they may have some weight, with my readers, in convincing them of the expediency of giving their earnest support to the Bill now proposed.

I remain, Gentlemen,

With great respect.

Your very obedient servant,
THOMAS STREET,

Philpot-Lane, London,
    15th April, 1818.

THOUGHTS, &c. &c.

THE local knowledge acquired by occasional residence, for many years past, in the Forest of Waltham and the neighbourhood, and its having been the favourite spot where I have indulged in occasional relaxation from professional pursuits, my attention has been drawn to the notice given of an intended application to Parliament for an inclosure of that and also of Hainault Forest, and the controversy which has taken place respecting such a proceeding has induced me to peruse the papers that have been published on the subject, and to reduce to writing a few observations thereon; and, although my remarks are intended to apply more particularly to the neighbourhood of Woodford, yet I think they will be found not inapplicable to the interests of the landed proprietors in general within the precincts of these Forests.

I, some time since, understood, from authority, the correctness of which I have no reason to doubt, that it was not the intention of the Crown to press for a general inclosure of these Forests, but merely to obtain a reasonable compensation (to be settled by the Commissioners under the proposed Act) for disafforesting both Waltham and Hainault Forests, and extinguishing the rights of the Crown therein. I hare considered the subject with much attention, and I confess that I could hardly have pictured to myself any thing so desirable to the owners of landed property in and adjoining to these Forests, as their being relieved from the rights of the Crown, rights from which, in point of fact, the Crown derives no sort of benefit; but, on the contrary, incurs an annual expense of £300, (as appears by the 15th Report of the Commissioners of Woods and Forests,) and which have been, for many years past, a continual source of complaint on the part of the land-owners and inhabitants. I was, therefore, much surprised, on perusing the resolutions passed, on the 26th November last, at a Meeting of the Freeholders and others, possessing landed property in the parish of Woodford, to find them so strongly deprecate the proposed inclosure.

As to the proposition respecting Hainault Forest:—the principal part of it, which is occupied by the growth of timber, is so low and swampy, that no human being would ever think of building in such a situation, and the land could not be brought into cultivation without an enormous expense in grubbing up the timber, and draining the soil. If, therefore, we give the Commissioners for the Inclosure credit for a reasonable degree of judgment and discretion, it is within this part of the Forest, so well calculated for the growth of timber, that they would undoubtedly appropriate the 2,000 acres to be inclosed as a nursery for that purpose, and for which it would be a situation peculiarly advantageous, on account of its easy communication with water-carriage and the dock-yard at Woolwich. I really cannot discover what injury could be done to the land-owners surrounding that spot, who, according to the plan proposed, would have a thousand acres of uninclosed land left subject only to the custom of the manor, within which their lands happen to lie, and totally free from the intervention of the forty days court; the frequent and inconvenient interference of which, in the exercise of the duty imposed on them of protecting the rights of the Crown, and preventing the deer being deprived of the herbage, has been so generally complained of by persons within its jurisdiction.

At the meeting held at Woodford, on the 26th of November last, certain resolutions were entered into, in which the persons passing them seemed to have been impressed with an idea, that a general inclosure was meant to be forced upon them, which, I believe, it never was in the contemplation of the Commissioners of Woods and Forests to attempt; and, in their eagerness to oppose such a measure, they have in my opinion, overlooked the beneficial effect which must necessarily result from a partial inclosure, and passed some resolutions founded on erroneous principles; for instance, the first resolution asserts "that no injury is sustained in the said parish by the depasturing of the deer." Now, it is most extraordinary how such an allegation could be made and sanctioned by the majority at such a meeting; for, to my certain knowledge, for upwards of thirty years past, the depredations committed by the deer have been a continual subject of complaint by the inhabitants of the parish of Woodford.

In the next resolution it is stated, that, "at the date of the 15th Report of the Commissioners of Woods and Forests, it appeared, by the evidence of Bamber Gascoyne, Esq. that the utter destruction of his Majesty's deer had, at that time, almost taken place, and that the persons present at that meeting had yet to learn that the number of deer had so materially increased, since that Report was made, as to render a total disafforestation or general inclosure necessary." If those gentlemen are really disposed to learn what the state of the deer now is in the Forest, they have only to ride about for a few hours in the retired parts of it, and they will see such herds as will easily convince them, that (presuming the Report, above alluded to, to be strictly accurate in this respect) the numbers must have increased prodigiously within the last twenty-five years; and this may be readily accounted for, when it is admitted that only twenty one brace annually are killed, for the use of persons claiming a right to venison from the Forests, (and I believe not a single head is destroyed for his Majesty's use,) and consequently the increase of these animals, which, in various parts of the Forests, may frequently be seen thirty or forty in a herd, must, in a very great degree, exceed the annual destruction. I will venture to assume, and I am sure I shall be borne out, on inquiry, that there are not less than 600 head of deer in Waltham and Hainault Forests; and, allowing but one-half of these to be does, they would, on a moderate calculation, now give an increase of 300 head annually, or at least of 200, allowing for those killed, destroyed, or lost, by various contingencies.

It is not in the power of the Crown, in opposition to the proprietors of land within any district, to enforce a general inclosure; and although, from local circumstances, there may be such well-founded objections to the measure as fully to justify the feelings of the gentlemen at that meeting in the resolutions they passed, yet it seems to me that, on the principle of commuting the rights of the Crown, and effecting inclosures to such an extent, only, as would satisfy the Crown for a sacrifice of those rights, they reject a proposal which it would be most desirable for all the parishes within the Forests, and for the parish of Woodford in particular, to have carried into effect. The quantity of waste land in the parish of Woodford is estimated at about 300 acres, and the Crown claims for its interests therein about one-third of that number. If a bill were brought into Parliament for inclosing such proportion only as the Commissioners should deem the Crown entitled to, or to allot a certain proportion to be specified in the Act, it could be productive of no advantage whatever to the parish of Woodford to have 100 acres of land inclosed for the growth of timber, nor would it answer the purpose of the Crown to have an inclosure of a similar, or, in many instances, a much less quantity allotted in different parishes for that purpose; a very different appropriation of such land would, I have no doubt, be much more desirable; and the plan I would suggest is, that the Commissioners should have a power of selling the lands allotted in lieu of the rights of the Crown, and that the Bill should contain clauses, directing the Commissioners to make their allotments in parcels of not less than two acres, but not exceeding five or ten, and preferring those situations where the proprietor of any dwelling-house or grounds should express to the Commissioners his assent to the inclosure of waste lying near or contiguous to such house or grounds, and that such owner should be allowed a right of pre-emption of the allotment so inclosed, at a price to be set thereon by two surveyors, one to be appointed on behalf of the Crown, and the other on the part of the purchaser; such surveyors, in case of disagreement, having power to elect a third, to decide between them. Now, supposing 100 acres to be so allotted, I would ask, if there are not twenty houses in the parish of Woodford, the owners of which would be glad to have an addition of five acres of contiguous waste inclosed; and if there are not, in every other parish within the Forest, proprietors of land who would be glad to have such a partial inclosure as would afford them an addition of a like quantity of land. It clearly appears to me, that an inclosure, carried into effect upon this principle, and to this extent, would be a most desirable measure for the proprietors of houses and lands in every parish on the Forest: and there should be a clause restraining the Commissioners from making inclosures within a certain distance of any dwelling-house, without the consent of the owner, so that no one should have the inclosure brought to his door, without his own consent. This plan would, in all probability, not occasion a single additional building; the 36,000 paupers, of whom so dreadful a picture has been drawn, (and whose numbers appear to have been calculated upon the visionary foundation of some antient adage,) would all vanish, and the new inclosures, which it is highly probable would, in most instances, be converted into ornamental grounds, and be adorned with new plantations, would add greatly to the bounty of the country; and a very abundant portion of waste would still be left to preserve the rural scenery, for which this district has been so much and so deservedly admired. The value of the landed properly, I have no doubt, instead of being deteriorated, by pursuing this system, would be very considerably increased.

Let us now look forward to the situation in which the proprietors of houses and land, in these Forests, would stand as to the remaining waste, which would become merely wastes of the respective manors, relieved from any rights of the Crown over them, and from the paramount power of the forty days court, which, of course, must cease with the extinction of the Crown's rights; and any proprietor wishing for an addition of one or two acres to his premises, (which in many instances, no doubt, it would be highly desirable to obtain,) might, on application to the Lord of the Manor, with the consent of the

Homage Jury, procure a grant thereof as copyhold, an advantage not now to be obtained on almost any terms: the right of Common, too, would be relieved from the necessity of withdrawing the cattle during the fence months, and be general through the year.

There is another circumstance mentioned in the Commissioners' Report, about the state of the timber, in the year 1783, which, I think, must have considerably changed since that period, namely, "that, out of 11,000 oaks, there were 2,700 fit for the use of the Navy." Now, I verily believe that, at the present time, not one-fourth of the number could be found fit for that purpose; and, as to the 7,000 young trees, mentioned in the same Report, there are scarcely any of them that have not, as they attained a certain age, been converted into, and are now become, old pollards; for the right of cutting fire-wood is, in the ideas of the lower sort of people, confirmed and increased, by preventing trees from becoming timber, and converting them to pollards, of which it is the common course of the country to cut the tops for fire-wood; and, in most parts of the Forest, the beauty of the scenery and utility of the timber are totally destroyed by the decapitation of the trees.

In the New Forest, in the Forest of Dean, and in Marlborough Forest, there is a great deal of beautiful forest scenery, where the practice of reducing the trees to pollards is not permitted; but, in much the greater part of Waltham Forest, the beauty is totally destroyed by this practice; and, therefore, it must be a most desirable measure, as regards the appearance of the country, to have the rights of cutting fire-wood totally abolished.

I have not entered into any wild speculations, but have confined myself to a plain and, I hope, intelligible statement of a plan that I now see reason to hope will be carried into effect, and, I have no doubt, will prove of real advantage to the proprietors of houses and lands within this district.

As many of my readers may not have seen the last Circular Letter, of the Surveyor of Woods and Forests, on the subject of the inclosure, and the Heads of the intended Bill, in which the plan submitted in the preceding pages is meant to be adopted, I have added copies, by way of Appendix.

I cannot easily imagine on what grounds any serious opposition can be attempted to the measure now proposed, unless the Commissioners of Woods and Forests are to be told that they shall keep and preserve Royal Forests and extensive and useless Wastes, with all the severity and arbitrary spirit of the barbarous days of William Rufus, on the one hand; or that, on the other, if they do adopt any species of inclosure, it shall be in rood [17] allotments, for the accommodation of cottagers and paupers,—the inevitable consequence of which would be that every parish in the Forest would be inundated with persons dependent on daily labour for subsistence, where employment for such numbers could not possibly be found, and they must, of necessity, become burthens to the several parishes in which they might thus be domiciled.

Viewing the subject, then, calmly and deliberately, with a mind wholly unbiassed either by local prejudices or party-spirit, I cannot conceive a more desirable medium than the plan intended to be carried into effect by the Bill now proposed, as it seems not easy to devise one that can more effectually meet the wishes, and bring to the very door of the proprietors of houses and land within the Forests a degree of accommodation and convenience—the want of which has been so long lamented, owing to the insuperable difficulties of obtaining any small inclosures or grants of land, under the existing system.

A clause was introduced into the Act of the 55th year of his present Majesty, relative to Crown Lands, whereby the Commissioners of Woods and Forests were enabled to sell the Rights of the Crown in any small parcels of land, within any of the Royal Forests, which adjoined or lay contiguous, or convenient to the lands of individuals, and were of little value for the growth of timber, or to sell the Rights of the Crown in and over lands belonging to any of his Majesty's subjects, lying within the limits aforesaid;—but the difficulties attending the procuring grants of land under this power were so great that it has been very little acted upon.

Whatever useful alterations or amendments in the proposed plan can be suggested, I have no doubt will meet with a fair and candid investigation by the Commissioners, and be made the subject of corrections, or additional clauses, when the Bill is before a Committee of the House of Commons.

I have heard the question asked by a proprietor of land, in allusion to the proposed plan, what do the Crown give us in lieu of the 9-32d parts, or 2810 acres we are to give up? The answer is plain; in the first place, you give the Crown nothing but what it had a right to before, and the Commissioners give up all the Rights of the Crown, over the remainder of the 9000 acres; and one may compare it to the common case of an agreement between the lord of a manor and the copyholders for an inclosure and enfranchisement of the whole, would not the lord be fairly entitled to one-third part, as a satisfaction for the rights he gave up, and would not the copyholders be remunerated by getting their copyholds converted to freeholds, and their commons to valuable inclosures; and, in this case, the remaining 23-32d parts, or 6190 acres, being discharged from the Rights of the Crown, may either be enjoyed as common, or may be inclosed at any future time, if the proprietors of land should agree in such a measure.—At present, the majority appear to be against a general inclosure; and, as far as the beauty of the country is at stake, I think they are right, for that certainly is an object of no small importance in a district so near the metropolis; but that will not be affected by an inclosure to the extent only proposed by the intended Bill.

APPENDIX.

Office of Woods, &c.
Whitehall-Place,
30th March, 1818.

SIR,

I am directed by the Commissioners of His Majesty's Woods, &c. to acquaint you, that since the date of my Circular Letter, in November last, stating the outlines of the measure then proposed for vesting in his Majesty certain parts of Hainault, Waltham, or Epping Forests, they have received various Memorials and Representations from, or on behalf of, the Lords of Manors, Freeholders, and others, having or claiming Rights over those Forests;—from those communications, it appears that an opinion has been very generally entertained, that it was in contemplation to COMPEL a Division and Inclosure in severalty of the whole of the Wastes within the boundaries of the said Forests, and that the greatest part of the objections, which have been stated to the proposals of the Commissioners, are founded upon misapprehension;—the Commissioners are, therefore, desirous that it should be distinctly understood, that it never was their intention to urge the measure of a general Inclosure of those Wastes contrary to the wishes of the majority of the Freeholders, and that their only object will be, to obtain for His Majesty separate Allotments of such extent in the whole, as shall be equivalent to his Rights and Interests in that Property; leaving the residue to be occupied by the Proprietors as they may think fit, freed and discharged from the Jurisdiction of the Forest Courts, from the Controul of Forest Officers, from the pasturage of the King's Deer, and from all other Forestal Rights of the Crown.

The Commissioners have, therefore, determined to confine their Proceedings to this Object, and having given the best Consideration in their power to the Communications and

Suggestions contained in the Memorials and Representations above referred to, I have received their Commands to send, for your information, the inclosed Heads of the Bill now intended to be proposed to Parliament, in which the Commissioners have modified their former Proposals, with a view to the interests and local convenience of the owners of Property in and adjoining those Forests, as far as they deem to be compatible with their public Duty.

It having been mentioned, in my former Letter, that a Public Meeting would probably be convened for the purpose of considering any details or matters of local convenience which it might have been desirable to settle, previous to the introduction of the Bill into Parliament, I am directed to state, that as the Measure is now intended to be confined to a separation of the Rights and Interests of the Crown from those of the Proprietors, it seems to the Commissioners, that any question which may arise respecting those Rights and Interests may be better discussed by Communications with them, or with their Solicitor, than they could be at any Public Meeting.

I have the honour to be,

SIR,

Your most obedient Servant,
A. MILNE.

WALTHAM, EPPING, OR HAINAULT FORESTS.

HEADS of the BILL proposed to be submitted to Parliament, in the present Session, for vesting in His Majesty certain Portions of the said Forests in lieu of his Forestal and other Rights, and for disafforesting the said Forests.

IT IS PROPOSED,

1st. THAT the Commissioners to be named as hereinafter mentioned shall be empowered and directed to set out and allot two-third parts of that portion of Hainault Forest, called *"King's Woods,"* to be for ever held by His Majesty in severalty, as a Nursery for Timber for the Navy, freed and discharged from all Rights of Common, and other Rights whatever, as a Compensation for the Right of Soil, and all Forestal and other Rights of His Majesty, or of those holding any Office or Offices under the Crown, in and over the other, or remaining third part of such Woods, except the Timber and Underwood growing thereon, which are to be reserved to His Majesty, and to be cut down and cleared away within three years after the passing the Act.

2d. THAT such remaining third part shall be possessed and enjoyed IN COMMON by the several persons who are now, or would have been, entitled to Rights of Common over the whole of the said Woods, if such proposed severance had not been made, freed and discharged from all Rights of Soil, and all Forestal and other Rights of His Majesty and his Successors therein, or of those holding any Office or Offices under the Crown, save as aforesaid.

3d. THAT the Commissioners shall be authorized and directed to set out and allot unto and for His Majesty in each and every of the other Parishes or Manors situate within the Forests, over which the Forestal Rights of His Majesty shall be found and ascertained to extend, so much of the open and waste Lands within each and every of such Parishes or Manors, (except the King's Woods aforesaid) as shall, quantity, quality, and situation considered, be equal to nine thirty-second parts of so much of the Waste Lands in each and every of such Parishes or Manors respectively as are within the Boundaries and Limits of the said Forest, and subject to the Forestal Rights of His Majesty as aforesaid, in satisfaction of such Forestal and other Rights in and over such Parishes respectively.

4th. THAT the Timber and Underwood now growing on such of the Allotments to be made to His Majesty, as are herein last described, shall be cut down and removed by the Parties now entitled to the same within three years after the passing of the Act, or shall be taken with the Allotment, and paid for by the Crown, according to the Valuation of the Commissioners under the Act, at the option of the party so entitled.

5th. THAT all the remainder of the Waste Lands within the said Forest not so alloted to His Majesty, shall remain for the benefit of the several Lords of Manors, Owners of Soil, and other Persons entitled to Rights of Common on the Forest, to be enjoyed IN COMMON as heretofore, according to their respective Rights and Interests therein, freed and discharged from the Jurisdiction of the Forest Court, all Rights of His Majesty, and his Successors, or of those holding any Office or Offices under the Crown.

6th. THAT the Allotments to be made to His Majesty shall be freed and discharged from all Rights of Common, of what nature or kind soever, and shall be in full Compensation and Satisfaction of all Forestal Rights, Claims, and Demands, whatsoever, of His Majesty, or of those holding any Office or Offices under the Crown, over any of the open and inclosed Grounds within the Limits or Perambulations of the Forest.

7th. THAT the Rights of His Majesty and His Officers in and over the Forest, and all Laws and Statutes now in force for protection of Deer, and for punishing Persons guilty of any Offences in breach of such Laws shall remain and continue in full force for the protection of the Deer within the regard of the Forest, and for the punishment of offences therein, until the 5th day of July, 1820.

8th. THAT the Commissioners of His Majesty's Woods, &c. shall, as soon as conveniently may be, after the passing of the Act, and before the said 5th day of July, 1820, at furthest, cause all the Deer in the said Forest to be destroyed or removed.

9th. THAT from and after the said 5th day of July, 1820, all right of keeping Deer, and all other Forestal rights and Privileges whatsoever, either of His Majesty, or of those holding any Office or Offices under the Crown, within, upon, and over, the said Forest, shall cease, determine, and be for ever extinguished; and the whole of the said Forest shall be thenceforth disafforested to all intents and purposes whatsoever.

10th. THAT from thenceforth all Grants of any Offices, Bailiwicks, Walks, and Lodges, and all Salaries, Gratuities, and Fees, payable or allowed in respect of the same, shall cease or determine: and that the several persons holding, or entitled to such Offices, shall be compensated for the Abolition thereof, by or out of the Allotments to be made to His Majesty, as aforesaid, the quantum and amount of which compensations shall be settled by Referees.

11th. THAT two Commissioners, one to be nominated on the part of His Majesty, and the other on the parts of the Lords of Manors, Owners of Soil, and other persons having rights of Common on the Forest, shall be appointed for carrying the Act into execution, and all requisite Provisions shall be comprised in the Act for the Appointment of Successors to such Commissioners, and for the Nomination of Surveyors, &c.

12th. THAT the Commissioners of His Majesty's Woods, &c. shall be empowered to sell or exchange all or any of the Allotments so to be made to or for His Majesty, as aforesaid, (except the Allotment of the King's Woods, as aforesaid).

13th. THAT in the setting out the Allotments of the said Waste Lands for His Majesty, the Commissioners for carrying the Act into execution shall, in each and every Parish, select such Portions as shall least interfere with the general range of Pasturage over the remaining Waste, and shall, as far as may be, have regard to the convenience and accommodation of the inhabitants; and, to that end, where notice shall be given within a time to be limited in the said Act, by any Owner or Occupier of any House or Land within the Forests to the said Commissioners, of his desire to have any Portion of the King's Allotment of the said Waste set out contiguous to his House, Garden or Pleasure Grounds, with an intent that he may become the Purchaser thereof at a fair Valuation, the said Commissioners shall, if the same can be conveniently done, set out a portion not exceeding five Acres of the Allotment for His Majesty in such Parish, as near and contiguous to the House of the Person giving such Notice as may be, and the same shall be sold to the Person so applying at a Valuation to be made thereof by the Commissioners. Or, if more than one Person shall give notice of their desire to purchase the same Lot, then such Lot shall be divided in portions to be ascertained, with reference to the extent and value of the Property to which it is proposed to be laid, and be offered to the Owners of such Property, in the portions so to be ascertained as aforesaid.

14th. THAT the Expenses of passing the Act shall be borne and paid by the Commissioners of Woods, on behalf of His Majesty, and also one half part of the Expenses of carrying the same into execution, and that the other half part shall he borne and paid by the Lords of Manors, Freeholders, and Parties entitled to Rights over the Waste, and shall be raised by the sale of such an Allotment of their residue of the Waste as shall be deemed sufficient for that purpose.

15th. THAT the Commissioners for carrying the Act into

execution shall be required to complete their Award, and all Proceedings under the Act, on or before the 5th day of July, 1820.

THE END.

FOOTNOTES.

[17] In allusion to every rood maintaining its man.

Milton Keynes UK
Ingram Content Group UK Ltd.
UKHW042258170324
439575UK00004B/330